A Family Culinary

Recipes to Remember

By

Margie G. Kuhn

COOKERY FOR CHILDREN.

*Observations on the Care of Children—Times of Giving Food important—
Duty of Mothers—Food for Infants—Milk—Porridge—Meats—
Vegetables—Puddings—To prepare Fruit—Rice and Apples—Fresh
Fruits—Blackberry Jam, &c.*

SOME preparations of food proper for the young have been given in the course of this work; nevertheless, we are sure a chapter on this important subject, so generally neglected in cookery books, will be welcomed by the judicious.

It is of great consequence to fix the times of taking food, as well as to regulate the quantity given to a child. The mother should, personally, attend to these arrangements; it is her province.

There is great danger that an infant, under 3 years of age, will be over-fed, if it be left to the discretion of the nurse. These persons, generally, to stop the screaming of a child, whether it proceed from pain, or crossness, or repletion (as it often does)—they give it something to eat—often that which is very injurious, to tempt the appetite; if it will only eat and stop crying, they do not care for the future inconvenience which this habit of indulgence may bring on the child and its mother.

Arrange, as early as possible, the regular times of giving food to your children, according to their age and constitution. Young infants require food every 2 hours when awake; after 3 months old, they may go 3 hours—then cautiously lengthen the time, as the child can bear it. But remember that all temperaments are not alike. Some of the same age may require more food than others. One rule, however, will apply to all —never give a child food to amuse and keep it quiet when it is not hungry, or to reward it for being good. You may as rationally hope to extinguish a fire by pouring on oil, as to cure a peevish temper or curb a violent one by pampering the appetite for luxuries in diet; and all the traits of goodness you thus seek to foster will, in the end, prove as deceptive as the mirage of green fields and cool lakes to the traveller in the hot sands of the desert.

"My children have very peculiar constitutions," said an anxious mother—"they are so subject to fevers! If they take the least cold, or even have a fall, they are sure to be attacked by fever." The family lived high, and those young children had a seat at the table, and were helped to the best and richest of everything. And their luncheon was cake and confectionary.

It was suggested to the mother that if she would adopt a different diet for those children, give them bread and milk morning and evening, and a plain dinner of bread, meat, and vegetables, their liability to fevers would be much lessened.

"My children do not love milk, and won't touch plain food"—was the answer, with a sort of triumphant smile, as though this cramming of her children with good things till the blood of the poor little creatures was almost in a state of inflammation, was a high credit to her good housekeeping.

But do not err on the other hand; and for fear your child should be over-fed, allow it insufficient nourishment. There is not in our country much reason to fear that such will be the case; the danger is, usually, on the side of excess; still we must not forget that the effects from a system of slow starvation are, if not so suddenly fatal as that of repletion, more terrible, because it reduces the intellectual as well as the physical nature of man, till he is hardly equal to the brutes.

In many parts of civilized and Christian Europe, the mass of the people suffer from being over-worked and under-fed; few may die of absolute starvation, but their term of life is much shortened, and their moral and intellectual powers dwarfed or prostrated.

"Under an impoverished diet," says Dr. Combe, "the moral and intellectual capacity is deteriorated as certainly as the bodily"—and he adverts to the work-house and charitable institution system of weak soups and low vegetable diet, and to the known facts that children brought up on such fare are usually feeble, puny, and diseased in body, and are at best but moderate in capacity.

The rational course seems to be, to feed infants, till about 3 years old, chiefly with milk and mild farinaceous vegetable preparations; a large portion of good bread, light, well-baked, and *cold*, should be given them; after that period, to proportion their solid food to the amount of exercise they are able to take. Children who play abroad in the open air, will require more hearty nourishment, more meat, than those who are kept confined in the house or school-room. From the age of 10 or 12 to 16 or 18, when the growth is most rapid and the exercises (of boys especially) most violent, a sufficiency of plain nourishing food should be given; there is little danger of their taking too much, if it be of the right kind and properly cooked. But do not allow them to eat hot bread, or use any kind of stimulating drinks.

Food for a Young Infant.—Take of fresh cow's milk 1 table-spoonful, and mix with 2 table-spoonsful of hot water; sweeten with loaf-sugar as much as may be agreeable. This quantity is sufficient for once feeding a new-born infant; and the same quantity may be given every 2 or 3 hours—not oftener—till the mother's breast affords the natural nourishment.

Thickened Milk for Infants, when 6 months old.—Take 1 pint of milk, 1 pint of water; boil it, and add 1 table-spoonful of flour.
Dissolve the flour first in half a tea-cupful of water; it must be strained in gradually, and boiled hard 20 minutes. As the child grows older, one-third water. If properly made, it is the most nutritious, at the same time the most delicate food, that can be given to young children.

Broth—Made of lamb or chicken, with stale bread toasted, and broken in, is safe and healthy for the dinners of children, when first weaned.

Milk—Fresh from the cow, with a *very* little loaf-sugar, is good and safe food for young children. From 3 years old to 7, pure milk, into which is crumbled stale bread, is the best breakfast and supper for a child.
For a Child's Luncheon.—Good sweet butter, with stale bread, is one of the most nutritious, at the same time the most wholesome articles of food, that can be given children after they are weaned.

Milk Porridge.—Stir 4 table-spoonsful of oatmeal, smoothly, into a quart of milk, then stir it quickly into a quart of boiling water, and boil up a few minutes till it is thickened: sweeten with sugar.

Obs.—Oatmeal, where it agrees with the stomach, is much better for children, being a fine opener as well as cleanser; fine flour in every shape is the reverse. Where biscuit powder is in use, let it be made at home; this, at all events, will prevent them getting the sweepings of the baker's counters, boxes, and baskets.[*]

Meats for Children.—Mutton, lamb, and poultry, are the best. Birds and the white meat of fowls, are the most delicate food of this kind that can be given. These meats should be slowly cooked, and no gravy, if made rich with butter, should be eaten by a young child. Never give children hard, tough, half worked meats, of any kind.

Vegetables for Children, Eggs, &c.—Their rice ought to be cooked in no more water than is necessary to swell it; their apples roasted, or stewed with no more water than is necessary to steam them; their vegetables so well cooked as to make them require little butter, and less digestion; their eggs boiled slow and soft. The boiling of their milk ought to be directed by the state of their bowels; if flatulent or bilious, a very little curry powder may be given in their vegetables with good effect—such as turmeric and the warm seeds (not hot peppers) are particularly useful in such cases.

Potatoes and Peas.—Potatoes, particularly some kinds, are not easily digested by children; but this is easily remedied by mashing them very fine, and seasoning them with sugar and a little milk.

When peas are dressed for children, let them be seasoned with mint and sugar, which will take off the flatulency.[*] Never give them vegetables less stewed than would pulp through a cullender.

Puddings and Pancakes for Children.—Sugar and egg, browned before the fire, or dropped as fritters into a hot frying-pan, without fat, will make them a nourishing meal.

Rice Pudding with Fruit.—In a pint of new milk put 2 large spoonsful of rice well washed; then add 2 apples, pared and quartered, or a few currants or raisins. Simmer slowly till the rice is very soft, then add 1 egg, beaten, to bind it. Serve with cream and sugar or molasses.

Hasty-Pudding—Made of Indian meal, and eaten in milk or with molasses, is nutritious and healthful food.

To Prepare Fruit for Children.—A far more wholesome way than in pies or puddings, is to put apples sliced, or plums, currants, gooseberries, &c., into a stone jar; and sprinkle among them as much Lisbon sugar as necessary. Set the jar in an oven or on a hearth, with a tea-cupful of water to prevent the fruit from burning; or put the jar into a sauce-pan of water till its contents be perfectly done. Slices of bread or Borne rice may be put into the jar, to eat with the fruit.

Rice and Apples.—Core as many nice apples as will fill the dish; boil them in light syrup; prepare a quarter of a pound of rice in milk, with sugar, and salt; put some of the rice in the dish, and put in the apples, and fill up the intervals with rice, and bake it in the oven till it is a fine color.

A nice Apple Cake for Children.—Grate some stale bread, and slice about double the quantity of apples; butter a mould, and line it with sugar paste, and strew in some crumbs, mixed with a little sugar; then lay in apples, with a few bits of butter over them, and so continue till the dish is full; cover it with crumbs, or prepared rice; season with cinnamon and sugar. Bake it well.

Fruits for Children.—That fruits are naturally healthy in their season, if rightly taken, no one, who believes that the Creator is a kind and beneficent Being, can doubt. And yet the use of summer fruits appears often to cause most fatal diseases, especially in children. Why is this? Because we do not conform to the natural laws in using this kind of diet. These laws are very simple and easy to understand. Let the fruit be ripe when you eat it; and eat it when you require *food*.

Now, nearly one half of the summer fruits used are eaten in an unripe or decaying state; more than half sold in the cities are in this condition. And this unhealthy fruit is often taken when no fruit is needed, after the full dinner, or for pastime in the evening. It is given to children to amuse them or stop their crying, when they are often suffering from repletion. Is it a wonder that fruits make people and children sick under such circumstances?
*

In the country, fruits in their season usually form part of the morning and evening meal of children with bread and milk; fresh gathered fruits; and they seldom prove injurious, eaten in this manner.

Fruits that have *seeds* are much healthier than the *stone* fruits, except perhaps peaches. But all fruits are better, for very young children, if baked or cooked in some manner, and eaten with bread. The French, who are a healthful people, always eat bread with raw fruit.

Apples and winter pears are very excellent food for children, indeed for almost any person in health; but best when eaten at breakfast or dinner. If taken late in the evening, fruit often proves injurious. The old saying that apples are *gold in the morning, silver at noon, and lead at night,* is pretty near the truth. Both apples and pears are often good and nutritious when baked or stewed, for those delicate constitutions that cannot bear raw fruit.

Much of the fruit gathered when unripe, might be rendered fit for food by preserving in sugar.

Ripe Currants are excellent for children. Mash the fruit, sprinkle with sugar, and with good bread let them eat of this fruit freely.

Blackberry Jam.—Gather the fruit in dry weather; allow half a pound of good brown sugar to every pound of fruit, boil the whole together gently for an hour, or till the blackberries are soft, stirring and mashing them well. Preserve it like any other jam, and it will be found very useful in families, particularly for children—regulating their bowels, and enabling you to dispense with cathartics. It may be spread on bread, or on puddings instead of butter; and even when the blackberries are bought, it is cheaper than butter. In the country, every family should preserve, at least, a half peck of blackberries.

To make Senna and Manna palatable.—Take half an ounce, when mixed, senna and manna; put it in half a pint of boiling water; when the strength is abstracted, pour into the liquid from a quarter to half a pound of prunes and 2 large table spoonsful of W. I. molasses. Stew slowly until the liquid is nearly absorbed. When cold it can be eaten with bread and butter, without detecting the manna, and is excellent for costive children.

Dr. J. F. Meigs' Receipt for Infants' Food.—Take a piece of gelatin, one inch square; dissolve it in half a gill of water over the fire; then add a gill of milk. When it comes to a boil, stir in half a tea-spoonful of Arrow Root, or double the quantity of boiled flour ball. When it is thoroughly boiled, take it off the fire and stir in two table-spoonfuls of cream. This may be given to a very young infant; and as it grows older, the quantity of the milk increased, and the food altogether made stronger,

* All the left bread in the nursery, hard ends of stale loaves, &c., ought to be dried in the oven or screen, and reduced to powder in the mortar.

* If they are old, let them be pulped, as the skins are perfectly indigestible by children's or weak stomachs.

THE DAIRY.

American Dairies—Care of Milk—Devonshire Method—To Make Butter—To Salt Butter—Making up Butter—Summer Butter—Winter Butter—To Cure Butter—Pickle for Butter—To Make Cheese—Cheshire—Stilton—New Cheese—To Keep Cheese—To Soften Old Cheese.

GENERAL REMARKS.—Always to make *good* butter or cheese shows great care and excellent judgment in the farmer's wife. When every department of the dairy is kept perfectly neat, there is hardly any exhibition of woman's industry more likely to make her husband proud, or gratify a beholder of good sense and benevolence, than the sight of a neat dairy-room filled with the rich, valuable productions which her skill has fashioned from the milk of the cow.

"The farmer's wife," says the accomplished Addison, "who has made nine hundred cheeses, and brought up half a dozen healthy children, is far more *amiable* in the eyes of unprejudiced reason, than the fine lady, who has made two millions of insipid visits, and propagated scandal from one end of the town to the other." The moral of this sentiment is true; rational employment, the industry either of hand or head, which produces benefit to society, is the real test of excellence in character,—and few American ladies desire any other standard.

The secret of success in the dairy is strict attention and scrupulous neatness in all its operations. The best time to make butter is in June, when the pastures are rich with clover, and September, when the *fall* feed is in its perfection. July and August are the months for cheese; then the rich new milk and cream cheeses are made.

Dairy work must be learned by practice, and requires as nice judgment and taste as cake-making. A few general directions may be followed to advantage; but there have not yet been any settled rules for this work which will insure good butter and cheese; it seems to depend very much on the skill of the individual manager, who does not often choose to communicate the secret of her infallible success. It is to be hoped that some of the intelligent women who are eminently successful in managing the dairy, will give the result of their experience—we might then frame receipts which would be very advantageous to the young farmer's wife, and of great benefit to the public; for it is a real calamity to have poor butter and cheese sent to market. Bad butter, particularly, is not only unhealthy, but it entirely spoils every good article of food in which it is mingled. Never purchase it, let it be ever so cheap. It is far better to eat molasses, or honey, or preserves, with bread, and use lard, beef drippings, suet, &c., for gravies and shortening, than to use bad butter.

To insure good butter, you must always scald your pans, pails, &c., in hot water, and then heat them by the fire, or in the hot sun, so that they may be perfectly sweet.*

Care of Milk.—When the milk is brought into the dairy, it should be strained into pans immediately, in Winter, but not till it is cool in Summer.

In Summer, milk should be skimmed in the morning, before the dairy becomes warm, and from 12 to 20 hours after it has been in the pans; in Winter, the milk should stand twice as long. In hot weather, the new milk should be scalded very gently, without boiling, as on a hot hearth, or in a brass kettle of water, large enough to receive the pan.

A spoonful of scraped horse-radish, put into each pan of milk will keep it sweet for several days.

Cream may be kept for 24 hours by scalding it; and if sweetened with loaf-sugar, powdered, it may be kept 2 days in a cool place. Cream for butter should be kept in a jar in the coolest part of the dairy; it should also be stirred often, and shifted every morning into a scalded vessel.

Devonshire Method of Scalding Milk.—This mode is very advantageous when the dairy is small, or the milk is produced in small quantities; for, by it, the cream may be kept for a long time, so that, instead of having butter rancid from being made with stale or sour cream, the butter is as sweet and fresh as if made from one day's cream. The trouble is trifling; pour the milk into a shallow brass or tin pan, and simmer it over a stove or wood fire until a bubble rises; take it off, let it stand till cold, when skim off the cream, and it may be more readily churned into butter than raw cream.

To Make Butter.—For large quantities of butter, the horizontal or barrel churn is the best; the upright or pump churn being adapted for making butter from the produce of a few cows only.

In Summer, you should churn 3 times a week, or twice a week at least; the churn ought then to be chilled with cold water before the cream is put into it, as well as whilst churning; and in Winter the churn should be soaked some time in warm water before it is used. Sweet cream requires 4 times as much churning as sour.

The quality of the butter depends much upon the temperature at which it is churned, which may be regulated by the aid of the thermometer. The cream should be kept at a moderate temperature. The greatest quantity of butter is obtained at 60 degrees, and the best quality at 55 degrees, in the churn just before the butter comes. At a higher heat, the butter comes quicker, but in less quantity, and of inferior quality But when the heat is below 50 degrees, it may be brought up to the temperature required by placing the churn in hot water but it will be better to wait; as butter thus hastened by hot water is worse than that which is turnip-flavored.

In the course of an hour's churning, more or less, according to circumstances, the butter will come, when the churn should be opened, and the butter taken out and put into a shallow pan or tub. The buttermilk should be set aside for pigs or for domestic purposes. The next point is to squeeze the milk from the butter, else it will not keep. This is usually done by spreading the butter in the tub, beating it with the hand, or a flat wooden spoon, and washing it repeatedly with clear spring water, until all milkiness disappears in the water which is poured off. Some persons maintain that the butter is injured by washing, and that the buttermilk should be beaten out of it with the hand, to be kept cool by frequently dipping it into cold water; or with a moist cloth, wrapped in the form of a ball, which soaks up all the buttermilk, and leaves the butter quite dry, No person should work butter who has not a very cool hand; the less it is handled the better, wherefore a wooden spoon or spatula, is preferable to the hand.

To Salt Butter.—A half ounce of salt to a pound of butter, is the rule. Add a little powdered sugar, say half a tea-spoonful, and less salt; the butter is sweeter and keeps better.

To make up Butter.—Butter requires more working in hot than in cold weather. When it is free from buttermilk, and salted, it should be divided into portions, if it is intended to be eaten soon. It should then be made into rolls of 2 pounds, or circular forms, to be impressed with some figure from wooden *print;* the rolls are made oblong, with four sides, slightly flattened by throwing the lump on a stone or board successively on each of the four sides, and then on the two ends.

To make prints, first work the butter into balls, and then press on it the wooden pattern: trim the sides up along the edge of the wood, and press the whole against a marble or wooden slab, so as to have the impression uppermost, and form a flattened cake. The wooden print is readily struck by holding it in the left hand, and giving a smart blow with the right upon it. A hole bored through the centre, prevents the butter sticking from the exclusion of the air.

Box-wood moulds, for shaping butter, may be bought at the turners'; they are in the form of fir-cones, pine-apples, shells, and swans, or in little tufts, coral branches, &c.

Butter in Hot Weather—Is usually soft and unsightly; to prevent which, set the dish in which it is kept to stand in cold spring-water, with a little saltpetre dissolved in it. Butter may also be kept cool in ice, or in water, but it should not stand long in the same water.

Butter in Winter.—To ensure good butter in Winter, wash and beat it free from milk, and work it up quickly with half an ounce of powdered saltpetre, and the same of loaf-sugar, powdered, to every pound of butter; pack it very closely in earthen jars or pots, and in a fortnight it will have a rich marrow flavor; it will keep for many months.

Obs.—To prevent butter made from the milk of a cow fed with turnips having their flavor, pour a pint of boiling water into the milk after milking: or, dissolve an ounce of saltpetre in a pint of water, and put about a quarter of a pint into the cream-pot with the cream from 3 good cows in a week.

To Cure Butter in the best manner.—The following receipt is from "The Housewife's Manual," a work said to have been prepared by Sir Walter Scott.

Having washed and beaten the butter free of buttermilk, work it quickly up, allowing a scanty half ounce of fine salt to the pound. Let the butter lie for 24 hours, or more; then, for every pound, allow a half ounce of the following mixture:—Take 4 ounces of salt, 2 of loaf-sugar, and a quarter of an ounce of saltpetre. Beat them all well together, and work the mixture thoroughly into the butter; then pack it down in jars or tubs. Instead of strewing a layer of salt on the top of the butter, which makes the first slice unfit for use, place a layer of the above mixture in folds of thin muslin, stitch it loosely, and lay this neatly over the top, which will effectually preserve it.

To Freshen Salt Butter.—Churn it anew in sweet milk, a quart to the pound. The butter will gain in weight.

To Improve Rancid Butter.—Wash it, melt it gradually, skim it, and put to it a slice of charred or hard-toasted bread or some bits of charcoal.

Pickle for Butter.—Allow half a pound of salt, an ounce of saltpetre, and half a pound of sugar to 3 quarts of water. Dissolve them together; scald and skim the pickle, let it be entirely cold, and then pour it over the butter.

Work out all the Butter-milk.—This must be done, or the butter will not keep well; and do not make the butter too salt.

Never put butter in a pine tub.

TO MAKE CHEESE.[*]

Pour out the milk, as soon as brought warm from the cow, into the cheese-tub; add a sufficient quantity of rennet to turn it, and cover it over with a cloth. This will make what is called a one-meal cheese. Let it stand till it is completely turned, when cut the curd with a cheese-knife or skimming-dish, into uniform pieces. Cover up the tub, and allow it to remain about 20 minutes. The pieces having settled, ladle off the whey, gently gather and press the curd towards the side of the tub, letting the whey pass through the fingers. Then break the curd as small as possible, and salt it to taste, either in the proportion of a handful of salt for every six gallons of milk, or about half an ounce to every pound of curd.

If the cheese be made, of two meals of milk, unless in very hot weather, a portion of the creamed milk of the first meal should be made scalding hot, and poured back into the cold; then, when well mixed, it should be poured into the cheese-tub; and the second meal of milk added warm from the cow. If, however, the milk be too hot, the cheese will be tough; as the tenderness of the curd depends upon the coolness of the milk.

In making very rich cheeses, the whey should be allowed to run off slowly; for, if forced, it might carry off much of the fat of the cheese. This happens more or less in every mode of making cheese. To collect this superabundant fat, the whey is set in shallow milk-pans, and an inferior kind of butter, called whey butter, is made from the cream or fat skimmed off.

If the cheese be colored, the substance used for coloring should be mixed with the milk at the time the rennet is put in. If herbs, as chopped sage, be added, they are mixed at the same time.

Cheshire Cheese.—In the cheese-making districts of Cheshire the milk is set together very warm, when the curd will be firm; it is then cut crosswise with a knife, in lines about an inch apart, about the depth of the knife-blade, so as to allow the whey to rise between the lines. The curd is then broken uniformly small, with a skimming-dish, and left with a cloth over it an hour to settle. Next, cut the curd into pieces of about an inch square, put it into a cloth, and then into a large wooden drainer, with a cover fitting inside it. Set it before a goad fire, and first put on the cover about half a hundred weight, so as to press the curd moderately; in 20 minutes, take out the curd, cut it still smaller, and press as before; and, in 20 minutes longer, cut it and press it again. Then put the curd into a tub or pan, cut it as small as birds' meat, and salt it; next put it into a cloth of thin gauze, into the chessel, or hoop, set it before a fire 12 or 15 hours and then put it into the press, taking it out from time to time and giving dry cloths, till, by the pressing, the cloths come oft quite dry; if the last cloth be of a finer texture, dipped in warm winter and wrung out, it will give the cheese a finer skin or rind.

Having taken the cheese out of the press, lay it on a dry shelf; at first turn and rub it daily with a dry cloth; and as the cheese becomes firm, turning and wiping twice a week will be sufficient. The following are good proportions: 6 drachms of anotta[*] to a cheese of 20 to 22 pounds; and 8 or 9 ounces of salt; 70 quarts of milk will make a cheese of the above weight, or about 3 quarts for each pound of cheese.

To Make Stilton Cheese.—The best season for making this rich cheese is from July to October. Add the cream of the preceding evening to the morning's milking, and mix them well together; great attention being paid to the even temperature of both, as the quality of the cheese rests much upon this part of the process. To make it in perfection, as much depends on the management of the cheese after it is made as upon the richness of the milk. The rennet should be very pure and sweet; when the milk is coagulated, do not break the curd, as in making other cheese, but take it out whole, drain it on a sieve, and press it very moderately. Then put the curd into a shape of the form of a cylinder (ten and a half inches deep, and 8 inches over,) and turn it 4 or 5 times a day into clean cloths. When it is sufficiently firm, bind a cloth or tape round it to prevent its breaking, and set it on a shelf. It should be occasionally powdered with flour, and plunged into hot water; this hardens the outer coat, and assists the fermentation, or ripening.

New Cheese.—Add a little hot water to 6 quarts of milk, warm from the cow, with rennet to turn it; when it is set, cut the curd, put it into a cheese-cloth, and hang it up; in half an hour, again break the curd, hang it up, and allow it to remain a few hours, when put it into the press; on the following day, take out the cheese, salt each side, and in 2 days it will be ready for use.

To Keep Cheese.—The keeping of cheese depends upon the mode of preparing it. Soft and rich cheeses are not intended to be kept long; hard and dry cheeses are best adapted to be kept. Of the first kind are all cream cheeses, and those soft cheeses called Bath cheeses, which are sold as soon as made, and if kept too long, become putrid. Stilton cheese is intermediate. Dutch, Cheshire, and Gloucestershire, and similar cheeses, are intended for longer keeping. The poorer the cheese is, the longer it will keep; and all cheese that is well cleared of whey, and sufficiently salted, may be kept for years. Cheese is often made from skim-milk, but it is never good.

If the milk be from cows fed on poor land, the addition of a pound of fresh butter in making a cheese will much improve it. A few cheeses thus made, in moderately warm weather, and when the cows are in full feed, will be advantageous for the parlor table.

To Soften Old Cheese.—If a cheese be much salted and very dry, wash it several times in soft water, and lay it in a cloth moistened with wine or vinegar; when it will gradually lose its saltness, and from being hard and dry, become soft and mellow, provided it be a rich cheese. This singular method of improving cheese, is generally practiced in Switzerland, where cheeses are stored for many years; and if they were not very salt and dry, they would soon be the prey of worms and mites. A dry Stilton cheese may be much improved by the above means.

Good Rules.—Never wash your cheese shelves; but always wipe them clean with a dry cloth, when you turn your cheese.

Do not heat the milk too hot; it should never, for new milk cheese, be more than blood-warm; be sure that your rennet is good, and do not use more than it requires to bring the curd.

Cover the pan or tub in which milk is set to coagulate, and do not disturb it for half an hour or more.

Cut the curd, when fully formed, carefully with a knife; never break it with a your hand; and be very particular, when draining it from the whey, not to squeeze or handle the curd; if you make the *white whey* run from the curd, you lose much of the richness of the cheese.

To Preserve Cheese Sound.—Wash in warm whey, when you have any, and wipe it once a month, and keep it on a rack. If you want to ripen it, a damp cellar will bring it forward. When a whole cheese is cut, the larger quantity should be spread with butter inside, and the outside wiped, to preserve it. To keep those in daily use moist, let a clean cloth be wrung out from cold water, and wrap round them when carried from table. Dry cheese may be used to advantage to grate for serving with macaroni or eating without. These observations are made with a view to make the above articles less expensive, as in most families where much is used, there is waste.

To Prevent Milk turning Sour in Hot Weather.—Add a little subcarbonate or potas of soda, which will keep milk sweet for some time.

* Such is the English way, and has been followed in our country till lately. A recent discovery is against this plan. It has been found that milk keeps longest in air-tight vessels; and that the *light* of the sun should never visit milk, butter, or cheese.

"Dairy rooms should be perfectly dark, and in the day time, when the sun shines, no air should be allowed to circulate through them. Air warmed in the sun will spoil butter and cream in 12 hours, if allowed to blow upon it.

HINTS FOR A HOUSEHOLD.

*Duties of the Mistress—A Word to Domestics—Domestic Economy—
    Washing Bay—To Purify Water—How to Wash Flannels,&c.—How to
    Clean Paint—Paper—Marble—Furniture—Pictures—Mirrors—
    Carpets—Brass—Glass.—Ironing—Baking,&c.&c.*

THE MISTRESS.—Far the greater proportion of households, throughout our whole country, are managed without the aid of much hired help, by the females of each family. The maxim, "If you would be well served, you must serve yourself," has considerable truth in it; at least those families who serve themselves, escape many vexations of spirit, because, if the work be not very well done, when we do it with our own hands, we are more apt to be satisfied. There are some sorts of domestic work, that of dairy work is one, which no hired help would be competent to discharge. This must be done by a wife or daughter, who feels a deep personal interest in the prosperity of her husband or father. Many of our farmers' wives are among the best housekeepers in the land, possessing that good sense, vigor of mind, native delicacy of taste or tact, and firm conscientiousness, which gift the character with power to attempt everything that duty demands. These are the "noble matronage" which our republic should honor. It is the sons of such mothers who have ever stood foremost to defend or serve their country—

"With word, or pen, or pointed steel."

One of the greatest defects in the present system of female education, is the almost total neglect of showing the young lady how to apply her learning so as to improve her domestic economy. It is true that necessity generally teaches, or rather obliges her to learn this science after she is married; but it would have saved her from many anxious hours, and tears, and troubles, if she had learned how to make bread and coffee, and cook a dinner before she left her father's house; and it would have been better still, if she had been instructed at school to regard this knowledge as an indispensable accomplishment in the education of a young lady.

I was once told by a lady of Boston, that, when she was married, she scarcely knew how a single dish should be prepared. The first day of her housekeeping, the cook came for orders—"What would she have for dinner?"

The lady told her, among other items, that she would have an apple pudding.

"How shall I make it?" was the question which the lady was unable to answer—she knew no more how to make a pudding than to square the circle. She evaded the question as well as she could, by telling the girl to make it in the usual way. But the circumstance was a powerful lesson on the inconveniences of ignorance to the housekeeper. The lady possessed good sense, and was a woman of right principles. She felt it was her duty to know how to order her help—that wealth did not free her from responsibility in her family. She set herself diligently to the study of cookery; and, by consulting friends, watching the operations of her servants, and doing many things herself, she has become a most excellent housekeeper.

For the young bride, who is entirely ignorant of her household duties, this is an encouraging example; let her follow it if she would be happy and respected at home. But it would be better to begin her lessons a little earlier; it is not every woman who has sufficient strength of mind to pursue such a rigid course of self-education. And no lady can be comfortable, unless she possess a knowledge of household work; if she need not perform it herself, she must be able to teach her help, otherwise she will always have *bad servants*.

I am aware that it is the fashion with many ladies to disparage Irish domestics, call them stupid, ignorant, impudent, ungrateful, the plagues of housekeeping. That they are ignorant, is true enough; it does require skill, patience, and judgment, to teach a raw Irish girl how to perform the work in a gentleman's family; but they are neither stupid nor ungrateful, and if they are taught in the right manner, they prove very capable, and are most faithful and affectionate domestics.

A friend of mine, who is just what a woman ought to be, capable of directing—even *doing*, if necessary—in the kitchen as well as shining in the drawing-room, hired one of these poor Irish girls, new from the land of the

Shamrock, who only understood the way of doing work in a hovel, yet, like all her class, she said, "Sure couldn't she do anything the lady wanted?" The lady, however, did not trust the girl to make any experiments, but went to the kitchen with her, and taught her, or rather did the work herself, and allowed the *help* to look on and learn by example, which for such is much more effectual than lectures. When the dinner was nearly ready, the lady retired to dress, telling Julia to watch the roast, and she would return soon, and show her how to prepare it for the table. We may imagine with what utter bewilderment the poor girl had been overwhelmed during this, her first lesson in civilized life. The names of the articles of furniture in the kitchen, as well as their uses, were entirely unknown to her; and she had seen so many new things done, which she was expected to remember, that it must have made her heart-sick to reflect how much she had to learn. But there was one thing she thought she understood—which was to cook potatoes. These were done, and she would show the lady she knew how to prepare them for the table.

When the lady returned, she found the girl seated on the floor, the potatoes in her lap, while she, with a very satisfied look, was peeling them with her fingers!

Are there not ladies who would have exclaimed—"Oh, the stupid, ignorant, dirty creature! She cannot be taught to do my work. I must send her away!" And away she would have been sent, irritated if not discouraged, and perhaps with out knowing a place where to lay down her head in this strange country.

My friend did not act in this manner—she expressed no surprise at the attitude of the girl, only quietly said—"That is not the best way to peel your potatoes, Julia—just lay them on this plate, and I will show you how I like to have them done."

That Irish girl remained a servant in the same family for 5 years, proved herself not only capable of learning to work, but willing and most devoted in the service of her mistress, whom she regarded with a reverence little short of what a Catholic feels for his patron saint.[*] And thus, if with patience and kindness these poor Irish girls are treated and taught, may good and faithful help be obtained.

But unless ladies know how the work should be done, and are willing to teach their domestics, they should not employ the Irish when they first arrive.

Those who do employ and carefully instruct this class of persons, perform a most benevolent act to the usually destitute exiles, and also a good service to the community, by rendering those who would, if ignorant, become a burden and a nuisance, useful and respectable members of society.

To educate a good domestic is one of the surest proofs that a lady is a good housekeeper.

A Word to Domestics.—Domestics in American families are very differently situated from persons of the same class in any other part of the world. Few enter the employment with any intention of remaining servants; it is only for a present resource to obtain a living and a little cash, so that they may begin business or house-keeping for themselves.

American *help*, therefore, should be very particular in their good behavior, and be careful to do by their employers as they will want *help* to do by them, when their turn to keep domestics shall arrive.

Never leave a good place because a little fault has been found with your work; it is a very great injury to a domestic to change her place often; she will soon have the name of being bad-tempered, and besides, she cannot gain friends; you must remain some time in a family before they will become attached to you. And if you are, as is generally the case, out of employment for a week before you go to a new place, you lose your time; and often have to pay for board too; thus a loss of 2 or 3 weeks' wages is incurred, because you will not bear to be reproved, even for a fault. What folly! thus to punish yourself for the sake of punishing your mistress, even if she did blame you without cause. The better way is to remain and behave so well that she shall be made to acknowledge your excellence; which she will be pretty sure to do, if she finds you faithfully try to please her.

Do not think it degrades you to endeavor to please your employer. It surely adds to your respectability, for it shows that you live with people you respect. You are bound to please your employers as far as you honestly can, while you receive your wages. No person hires a domestic to be idle, cross, or disrespectful. It is worse than theft to take wages from your employers which you must know you have not earned, if you have been unfaithful, impertinent, and quarrelsome, and made them constant trouble.

Resolve, therefore, when you go as *help*, to prove *help* indeed; which you will be, if you practice the following rules:—

Always treat your employers with respect.

Be faithful and honest in managing all that they entrust to you.

Be kind and obliging to every body, particularly to all the domestics of the family.

In a word—do to others in all things, as you would wish them to do by you in similar circumstances.

If you conduct thus, you will, though working in the kitchen, be as really respectable and independent as the lady in the parlor. In truth, she will be more dependent on your assistance than you will be on her for employment, and she will feel this, and treat you with the consideration and kindness which your merit deserves. But do not presume on this favor, and grow slack and careless. As long as you find it necessary to receive wages, be conscientious to perform all your duties as help.

Never think any part of your business too trifling to be well done.

The foregoing are general rules; a few particular directions may be needed.

One of the faults which a cook should most seriously guard against, is bad temper. She has a good many trials. Her employment, in the summer season, is not a pleasant or healthy one—obliged, as she is, to be over the hot fire, and confined, often, in a dark, close kitchen. Then she sometimes has a difficult lady to please, who does not know when the work is well done, and often gives contradictory or impracticable orders.

And the other domestics frequently interrupt the arrangements of the cook; or, she is not furnished with proper implements and articles. All these things try her patience, and if it *sometimes* fails, we ought not too much to blame her. But she need not be always *cross*. And she should remember, too, her privileges—mistress of the kitchen, the highest wages, and, if she conducts well, the favorite always of her employers.

It is in the power of the cook to do much for the comfort and prosperity of be family. If she is economical and conducts with propriety, the whole establishment goes on pleasantly; but if she is cross, *intemperate*, and wasteful, the mischief and discomfort she causes are very great. Never let the family have reason to say—"The cook is always cross!"

Intemperance is said to be the failing of cooks, oftener than of other domestics. It is a vice which, if persisted in, will soon destroy the character and usefulness of the cook. Every one who desires to sustain a respectable station in her employment, must abstain totally from spirituous liquors. "Touch not, taste not, handle not." It is poison to your blood; it is death to your reputation, if not to your body and soul.

Country girls who come to the cities as help, because they can there obtain large wages, should be careful in their diet. Remember that as you cannot take so much exercise in the open air, you must live sparingly at first, or the change will injure your health. And all that injures the health, injures also the bloom and beauty of youth.

To take a young woman, one of our farmer's daughters, from the free, pure air of the country, and confine her in the hot kitchen, often under ground, of one of our crowded city establishments, is such a change, that unless she is very particular in her care of herself, will soon cause her to look old, haggard, and disagreeable. Her hair will be often matted with sweat and dust, and her complexion like a mummy. To avoid these unpleasant results, let the cook, from the first, adopt the following rules:—

1st. Eat regular meals, instead of tasting of every good thing you cook, till you have no appetite for food.

2d. Keep your sleeping room well aired, and your skin clean.

The best way is to wash yourself thoroughly when going to bed; comb your hair also, and wear a night-cap or handkerchief on your head. The next morning, you will only require to smooth your hair, not take it down, and wash your face and hands. It would look neater, and keep your hair much smoother, if you would wear a cap or handkerchief while at work, as English servants do.

Let your dress be of good, durable materials, that will wash well; keep it clean as possible, and always wear an apron.

In the afternoon, when the work is done, then you can wash and dress as neatly as you choose, only remember that a domestic in a showy, flimsy gown, and decked out with pinchbeck rings and ear ornaments, always makes a ridiculous figure in the eyes of every sensible person; because such persons see that you are spending your hard-earned wages for that which really does you no good.

Keep your kitchen, and all the utensils, clean and neat as possible. Sweep the chimney often, with an old broom kept for the purpose, so that no soot may collect to fall down on the dishes at the fire, and be sure that the hearth is neat as a table.

Always have plenty of hot water ready; and take care that your wiping cloths are washed every day.

The three rules you must follow, if you would always have your work done well, are these:—

" Do every thing at the proper time.

Keep every thing in its proper place.

Use every thing for its proper purpose."

If your mistress professes to understand cookery, the best way will be to follow her directions; if you find the dish is not so good as when cooked in your own way, respectfully ask her to let you try once alone. But never be angry or pout when you are told how your employer wishes to have the work done.

The great fault of the Irish *help* is, that they undertake to do what they have never learned. They will not acknowledge their ignorance; if they would do this, and patiently try to learn, they would soon, with their natural quickness, become good cooks—if they have good teachers. And what a privilege and blessing it is to a poor Irish girl, who has only lived in a hovel, with scarcely an article of furniture, save the pot "to boil the praties," to be instructed in household work! It is really a fortune to her; she can then always have good places and good pay, and soon clothe herself well, and lay up money.

There are benevolent and sensible ladies who do act thus kindly by the Irish girl; not only teach her how to work in the kitchen, but teach her needlework, and instruct her in reading and writing.

If you have had such a kind mistress, my poor girl, for the honor of old Ireland be grateful and faithful to your benefactress; and show yourself worthy to be the mother of American citizens; for to such good fortune your children, should you marry, will be entitled.

There is no danger that our domestics will have too much ambition, if it be of the right kind—the ambition of doing their duty as faithful, capable *help,* while they continue to work for others. But I would wish every young female domestic to *hope* that she may some time be mistress of her *own house;* and I would urge her to improve every opportunity she has of learning the best and most prudent manner of doing all kinds of work. Then she will be fitted to make her husband happy, and bring up her children to be respectable members of society.

One of the most certain evidences that she is worthy to enjoy prosperity, is her faithfulness to promote the interest of those for whom she works. If she is really trustworthy, she will show it in her conduct.

There is a class of cooks who cannot be trusted; every thing they dare take is slyly carried out of the house, and given to their friends; and they go on with this system of pilfering till they are turned away from every respectable place.

Do not be tempted to begin this system, nor think that the broken bits, which the family may not need, belong to you. The mistress of the house must manage these charities; ask her, and if she give you leave to dispose of the broken pieces be very careful not to *make fragments* unnecessarily for the sake of giving them to your poor relations.

Act, in all these things, as you would if your employer was looking on you; and forget not that One, to whom you are more responsible than to any earthly master or mistress, is constantly watching you.

Domestic Economy.—If you would practice this economy to the greatest advantage, be regular in the arrangement of your work, punctual in preparing your meals, and take good care that *nothing is wasted.*

It is best to have the washing done on Mondays, if this can be managed without encroaching on that rest from labor which the holy Sabbath should always bring, as well to the domestics as to every other member of a Christian family. But whether Monday or Tuesday be the day, let it be fixed, and the washing never omitted when it is *possible* to have it done. The next morning, *early,* should be the time to begin ironing, so that the clothes may have time to be aired and put away before night.

Mend clothes *before* washing, except stockings; these can best be darned when clean.

Soft water is indispensable to the washerwoman; rain or river water is the best. If you have good water, do not use soda; it gives a yellowish tinge to the clothes. If you buy your soap, it is most economical to use hard soap for washing clothes, and soft soap for floors, &c.

To Purify Water.—A large spoonful of powdered alum stir red into a hogshead of impure water will, after the lapse of a few hours, precipitate the impurities, and give it nearly the freshness and clearness of spring water. A pailful may be purified with a tea-spoonful of alum.

Water-casks should be well charred before they are filled, as the charcoal thus produced on the inside of the cask keeps the water sweet. When water, by any accident, becomes impure and offensive, it may be rendered sweet by putting a little fresh charcoal in powder into the vessel, or by filtering the water through fresh-burnt and coarsely powdered charcoal.

Flannels—Should be washed in clean hot suds in which a little bluing has been mingled; do not rinse them. Woollens of all kinds should be washed in hot suds.

Colored Dresses.—Turn the inner side out, and wash them in cold water, in which a little boiled soap is well mixed; rinse them well in clean cold water, and the last time with a little salt in the water; and dry them in the shade. They should be washed and dried with as much expedition as possible.

Mildew Stains—Are very difficult to remove from linen. The most effectual way is to rub soap on the spots, then chalk, and bleach the garment in the hot sun.

Ink and Iron Mould—May be taken out by wetting the pots in milk, then covering them with common salt. It should be done before the garments have been washed. Another way to take out ink is to dip it in melted tallow. For fine, delicate articles, this is the best way.

Fruit and Wine Stains.—Mix 2 tea-spoonsful of water and 1 of spirit of salt, and let the stained part lie in this for 2 minutes; then rinse in cold water. Or wet the stain with hartshorn.

To Wash Carpets.—Shake and beat it well; lay it upon the floor, and tack it firmly; then with a clean flannel wash it over with 1 quart of bullock's gall, mixed with 3 quarts of soft cold water, and rub it off with a clean flannel or house-cloth. Any particular dirty spot should be rubbed with pure gall.

To Sweep Carpets.—The oftener these are taken up and shaken, the longer they will wear, as the dust and dirt underneath grind them out. Sweep carpets with a stiff hair brush, instead of *an old corn broom*, if. you wish them to wear long on look well. At any rate, keep a good *broom purposely* for the carpet.

To Clean Paint.—Put a very little pearl-ash, or soda, in the water to soften it, then wash the paint with flannel and soft soap; wash the soap off, and wipe dry with a clean linen cloth.

To Clean Paper Walls.—The very best method is to sweep off lightly all the dust, then rub the paper with stale bread—cut the crust off very thick, and wipe straight down from the top then begin at the top again, and so on.

To Polish Mahogany Furniture.—Rub it with *cold drawn linseed oil,* and polish by rubbing with a clean dry cloth, after wiping the oil from the furniture. Do this once a week, and your mahogany tables will be so finely polished that hot water would not injure them. The reason is this, linseed oil hardens when exposed to the air, and when it has filled all the pores of the wood, the surface becomes hard and smooth like glass.

To take Ink out of Mahogany.—Mix in a tea-spoonful of cold water, a few drops of oil of vitriol; touch the spot with a feather dipped in the liquid.

To Clean Pictures.—Dust them lightly with cotton wool, or with a feather brush.

To Clean Mirrors.—Wipe them lightly with a clean bit of sponge or fine linen that has been wet in spirits of wine, or in soft water; then dust the glass with fine whiting powder; rub this off with a soft cloth—then rub with another clean cloth, and finish it with a silk handkerchief. Dust the frames with cotton wool.

To Clean Straw Carpets.—Wash them in salt and water, and wipe them with a clean dry cloth.

To Clean Marble.—Pound very finely a quarter of a pound of whiting and a small quantity of stone blue; dissolve in a little water one ounce of soda, and mix the above ingredients carefully together with a quarter of a pound of soft soap; boil it a quarter of an hour on a slow fire, carefully stirring it. Then, when quite hot, lay it with a brush upon the marble, and let it remain on half an hour. Wash it off with warm water, flannel, and a scrubbing brush, and wipe it dry.

To Clean Freestone.—Wash the hearth with soap, and wipe it with a wet cloth. Or rub it over with a little freestone powder, after washing the hearth in hot water Brush off the powder when dry.

To Black a Brick Hearth.—Mix some black lead with soft soap and a little water, and boil it—then lay it on with a brush. Or mix the lead with water only.

To Clean Brass.—Rub it over with a bit of flannel dipped in sweet oil—then rub it hard with finely powdered rotten stone —then rub it with a soft linen cloth—and polish with a bit of wash leather.

Rub *creaking hinges* with soft soap.

To Prevent the Smoking of a Lamp.—Soak the wick in strong vinegar, and dry it well before it is used.

Glasses should be washed and rinsed in cold water, and the water wiped off with one cloth; then rub dry and clean with another.

Cut Glass should be rubbed with a damp sponge dipped in whiting, then brush this off with a clean brush, and wash the vessel in cold water.

An Ironing Board, Sheets, and Holders, should always be kept purposely for the ironing. A small board, 2 feet by 14 inches wide, covered with old flannel, and then with fine cotton, is handy to iron small articles on.

Isinglass is a most delicate starch for fine muslins. When boiling common starch, sprinkle in a little fine salt; it will prevent its sticking.

Some use sugar.

Bed Linen should be well aired before it is used. Keep your sheets folded in pairs on a shelf—closets are better than drawers or chests for linen, it will not be so likely to gather damp.

Hair, or even Straw Mattresses, are more healthy to sleep on than feather beds. Never put children on these heating beds. Keep your sleeping rooms very clean and well aired; and do not cumber them with unnecessary furniture.

Bed Curtains are unhealthy, because they confine the air around us while we are asleep.

Bread.—One of the most important household rules is, not to eat new bread; for it is expensive and unwholesome, and does not afford near so much nourishment as bread 2 or 3 days old.

Baking.—When baking is done twice a week, Wednesdays and Saturdays should be chosen; if only once a week, Saturday is the best, because it allows of preparation for the Sunday dinner—a pudding can be baked—and meat, too, if the family have a *real* desire of keeping the day for that which it was evidently intended, rest from worldly care, as well as for moral and religious improvement.

Old Bread may be made almost as good as new by dipping the loaf in cold water, then putting it in the oven after the bread is drawn, or in a stove, and let it heat through.

How to keep Various Things.—Crusts and pieces of bread should be kept in an earthen pot or pan, closely covered, in a dry cool place.

Keep fresh lard and suet in tin vessels.

Keep salt pork fat in glazed earthen ware.

Keep yeast in wood or earthen.

Keep preserves and jellies in glass, china, or stone ware.

Keep salt in a dry place.

Keep meal in a cool, dry place.

Keep ice in the cellar or refrigerator, wrapped in flannel.

Keep vinegar in wood or glass.

Housekeepers in the country must be careful that their meats are well salted, and kept under brine.

Sugar is an admirable ingredient in curing meat, butter, and fish.

Saltpetre dries up meat—it is best to use it sparingly.

To Preserve Eggs.—Cover the bottom of a small tub or cask with coarse salt—then place a layer of fresh eggs, standing *upright* on the large end—cover these with salt—then put another layer of eggs; and so on, till the tub is full. Keep it in a cool, dry place, and the eggs will remain good for a year. The last layer should be of *salt*, and an inch in thickness.

In the summer season, when eggs are not put in salt, they should be *turned* every day. Rubbing them over with butter or oil is said to make them keep fresh for several weeks.

* Julia only left her mistress to be married; she is now the good wife of a respectable mechanic.

OF DINNER PARTIES AND CARVING.

Rules for a Dinner Party—Carving—Its Importance—How to Carve Fish— Beef—Veal—Mutton—Lamb—Pork—Ham—Roast Pig—Turkey— Goose—Fowls—Pigeons—Tea Table.

MANAGEMENT OF A DINNER.—As a dinner affords the best proof of the management of a household, a few hints upon the subject may be useful to the heads of families.

The comfort of dinner-guests depends much upon the proper regulation of the temperature of the dining-room. In hot weather, this may be effected by ventilation and blinds. In winter, there is little difficulty to accomplish this with a bright blazing fire, and due care.

In families where a dinner is seldom given, it is better to hire a cook to assist in dressing the dinner, than to engage an uninformed person.

In selecting dinners, you should provide for the party such dishes as they are not most used to, and those articles which you are most in the way of procuring of superior quality.

Large dinner-parties, as 14 or 16 in number, are rarely so satisfactory to the entertainer or the guests as small parties of 6 or 8 persons. The latter, especially, are pleasant numbers.

Everything that unites elegance with comfort, should be attended to, but elegance ought to give way at all times to comfort. Two or three cloths make the table look much handsomer; and it is astonishing how meagre to an eye accustomed to that style, a table with only one appears; but this may be easily obviated, if the cloth is not removed during the service by having a stout coarse one under it, or a scarlet cloth under a fine thin damask, gives it an imperceptible glow; but, if such is used, the cloth must not be taken off, as nothing can took well in removing but linen. A scarlet cloth, fitted to the table, and laid between the table-cloths, preserves the polish, as well as adds to the appearance.

Finger Glasses, half filled with water, should be got ready to be set upon the table with the dessert.

Bread should never be cut less than one inch and a half for dinner.

To ensure a well-dressed dinner, provide enough, and beware of the common practice of having too much. The table had better appear rather bare than crowded with dishes not wanted, or such as will become cold before they are partaken of. This practice of overloading tables is not only extravagant but troublesome. The smaller the dinner, when sufficient, the better will be the chance of its being well cooked.

Vegetables, in abundance and well dressed, are important in a dinner; and it is a good plan to serve a fresh supply with each dish, to ensure them hot. In France, more attention is paid to the dressing of vegetables than in this country or in England; and the French, consequently, produce these cheap luxuries in high perfection.

Before a dish is placed upon the table, its sauces and vegetables should be set in their proper places.

Between the serving of each dish should be a short interval, which will not only be pleasant to the guests, but will give time to the cook and attendants.

There should be a reserve of sauces as well as of vegetables; for nothing lessens the enjoyment of a dinner so much as a short supply of these adjuncts.

A chief point to be attended to for a comfortable dinner is, to have what you want, and when you want it. It is vexatious to wait for first one thing and then another, and to receive these little additions, when what they belong to is half or entirely finished.

One or more sets of cruets, according to the size of the party, should be placed upon table; the cruets should contain such articles as are continually wanted, and special attention should be paid to the freshness of their contents, as of fish sauces.

Much money is often unnecessarily expended in pastry and denseness. A few kinds of ripe fruit, in season, and not forced, are sufficient; though the morning is the best time for eating fruit.

Wines should vary with the seasons; light wines are best in summer; in winter, generous wines are preferred. White wine is drunk with white meats, and red with brown meats. Light wines are suitable to light dishes, and stronger wines to more substantial dishes. In summer, wine and water, cooled by a piece of ice being put into it, is a luxury; as is also a bottle of iced water (the best beverage) and bottled porter iced.

Wine is often set upon the table before it is wanted, for show; so that it loses its proper temperature before it is required to be drunk.

Do not press persons to eat more than appears agreeable to them, nor insist upon their tasting any particular dish.

It is a good custom to send coffee into the dining-room before the gentlemen leave the table. The hour for sending in the coffee should be previously appointed, so that the bell need not be rung for it. Two or three hours are a proper interval between the dinner hour and coffee.

Servants who wait at table should wear clean white linen gloves.

There are a few points of the etiquette of a dinner-party, which it may be useful to particularize.

The members of the party having assembled, the master or mistress of the house should point out which lady each visitor is to take into the dining room, the married having precedence of the single.

The lady of the house should take the head of the table, and be supported by the two gentlemen of the most consideration, who should assist her to carve. The gentleman of the house should take the bottom of the table, and on each side of him should be seated the two ladies whose age or station gives them precedence.

As well-bred people arrive as punctually as they can to the appointed hour, the dinner should not be kept waiting after that time.

In serving soup, one ladleful to each plate is sufficient.

A knife applied to fish is likely to spoil the delicacy of its flavor; so that a slice only should be used in helping fish.

Do not pour sauce over meat or vegetables, but a little on one side. In helping at table, never employ a knife where you can use a spoon.

In giving dinners, avoid ostentation, which will not only be very expensive, but will make your guests uncomfortable. Again, it is not merely the expense, but the trouble and fuss of dinner-giving on the extravagant system, that checks the extended practice of giving dinners, and imposes a restraint upon sociable enjoyment.

ON CARVING.

One of the most important acquisitions in the routine of daily life is the ability to carve well, and not only well but elegantly. It is true that the modes now adopted of sending meats, &c. to table are fast banishing the necessity for promiscuous carving from the elegantly served boards of the wealthy; but in the circles of middle life, where the refinements of cookery are not adopted, the utility of a skill in the use of a carving knife is sufficiently obvious.

Moreover, the art of carving is a very requisite branch of domestic management; it not only belongs to *the honors of the table*, but is important in an economical point of view; for a joint of meat ill carved, will not serve so many persons as it would if it were properly carved.

Ladies ought especially to make carving a study; at their own houses they grace the table, and should be enabled to perform the task allotted to them with sufficient skill to prevent remark, or the calling forth of eager proffers of assistance from good natured visitors near, who probably would not present any better claim to a neat performance.

In the first place, whatever is to be carved should be set in a dish sufficiently large for turning it if necessary; but the dish itself should not be moved from its position, which should be so close before the carver as only to leave room for the plates. The carving knife should be light, sharp, well-tempered, and of a size proportioned to the joint, strength being less required than address in the manner of using it. Large solid joints, such as ham, fillet of veal, and salt beef, cannot be cut too thin; but mutton, roast pork, and the other joints of veal should never be served in very slender slices.

There are certain choice cuts, or delicacies, with which a good carver is acquainted; among them are the sounds of rod-fish, the thin or fat of salmon, the thick and fins of turbot; the fat of venison, lamb and veal kidney, the pope's eye in a leg of mutton, the ribs and neck of a pig; the breast and wings of a fowl, the legs and back of a hare, and its ears being by some persons considered a great delicacy; the breast and thighs (without the drumsticks,) of turkey and goose, the wings and breast of game, and the legs and breast of ducks.

Fish should be helped with a silver slice or trowel, care being taken not to break the handsome flaky pieces; a portion of the liver and roe should be served to each person.

Much of the enjoyment of the party will depend on the stuffing, gravies, sauces, &c., being fairly apportioned to each plate.

By aid of the following instructions, occasional practice, and by closely observing "good carvers," the learner may soon become proficient in this important branch of the honors of the table.

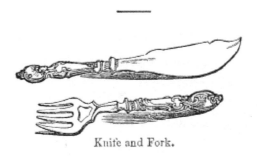

Knife and Fork.

Fish.—The carving of fish calls for but little observation, as it is always cut with a silver trowel, or a knife and fork made for the purpose, and should never be approached by steel; but, in helping it, care should be taken to avoid breaking the flakes, which should be kept as entire as possible.

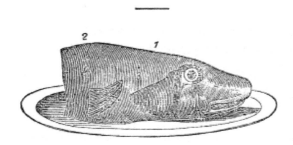

Cod's Head and Shoulders.—Take off slices, quite down to the bone, in the direction from 1 to 2, and as low as 3. With each slice of fish give a piece of the sound, which lies under neath the back-bone and lines it, and may be found by passing the slice under the bone. A few choice parts are in and about the head, as the soft part about the jaw-bone, and the palate and tongue, to be taken out with a spoon.

Salmon, and all short-grained fish, should be cut lengthwise, and not across; portions of the thick and thin being helped together.

Haddock is served like cod—but the head is worthless.

Mackerel are commonly served up head to tail, and a slice cut lengthwise from the bone.

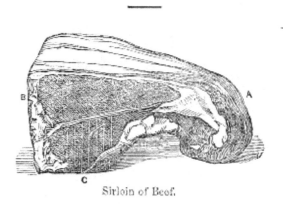

Sirloin of Beef.

Sirloin of Beef.—The under part of the sirloin should be first served, and carved, as indicated in the engraving, across the bone. In carving the upper part the same directions should be followed as for the ribs, carving either side, or in the centre, from A to B, and helping the fat from D.

Ribs of Beef—The best manner of carving this joint is to cut across the bone, commencing in the centre, and serving fat from A, as marked in the engraving of the *sirloin*. Another way, is to carve the slices from A to C, commencing either in the centre of the joint or at the sides. When the bones are removed, and the meat formed into a fillet, it should be carved as a round of beef.

A Round (Buttock) or Aitch Bone of Beef—Is usually boiled, and requires no print to point out how it should be carved. A thick slice should be cut off all round the buttock, that your friends may be helped to the juicy and prime part of it. The outside thus cut off, thin slices may then be cut from the top; but as it is a dish that is frequently brought to table cold a second day, it should always be cut handsome and even. When a slice all round would be considered too much, the half, or a third, may be given with a thin slice of fat. On one side there is a part whiter than ordinary, by some called the white muscle. In some places, a buttock is generally divided, and this white part sold separate, as a delicacy; but it is by no means so, the meat being coarse and dry; whereas the darker colored parts, though apparently of a coarser grain, are of a loosen texture, more tender, fuller of gravy, and better flavored; and men of distinguishing palates ever prefer them.

Fillet of Veal—Should be cut in thin, smooth slices, with a little fat to each; cutting also a thin slice from the stuffing, which lies within the flap. The brown outside is much liked by some persons.

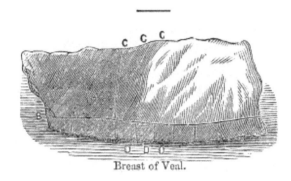

Breast of Veal.

The Breast of Veal.—Separate the ribs from the brisket, cutting from A to B; these small bones, which are the sweetest and mostly chosen, you will cut them as at D D D, and serve; the long ribs are divided as at c c c, and having ascertained the preference of the person, help accordingly; at good tables the scrag is not served, but is found, when properly cooked, a very good stew.

Loin of Veal.—This joint is sent to table served as a sirloin of beef. Having turned it over, cut out the kidney and the fat, return it to its proper position, and carve it as in the neck of veal, from B to A; help with it a slice of kidney and fat. The kidney is usually placed upon a dry toast when removed from the joint.

Shoulder of Veal—Is sent to table with the under part placed uppermost. Help it as a shoulder of mutton, beginning at the knuckle end.

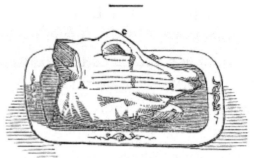

Half of Calf's Head.

Calf's Head.—There is much more meat to be obtained from a calf's head by carving it one way than another. Carve from A to B, cutting quite down to the bone. At the fleshy part of the neck end you will find the throat sweetbread, which you can help a slice of with the other part; you will remove the eye with the point of the knife and divide it in half, helping those to it who profess a preference for it; there are some tasty, gelatinous pieces around it which are palatable. Remove the jaw-bone, and then you will meet with some fine flavored lean; the palate, which is under the head, is by some thought a dainty, and should be proffered when carving.

Leg of Mutton.—The under or thickest part of the leg should be placed uppermost and carved in slices moderately thin. Many persons have a taste for the knuckle, and this question should be asked, and if preferred should be assisted. When cold, the back of the leg should be placed uppermost, and thus carved.

A leg of Lamb—Is carved as a leg of mutton. A leg of mutton or lamb, roasted or boiled, should be laid in the dish back downwards.

A Shoulder of Mutton—Affords a variety of cuts, fat and lean, and should be lain in the dish back uppermost. The leaner parts should be cut straight to the bone, from 1 to 2; the most delicate slices, however, may be cut on each side of the blade bone, 3 to 4; the finest fat lies at 5, and should be out in thin slices. The under-side affords many nice cuts, of fat and lean intermixed. The most tender of the lean is under the blade-bone, and is called the oyster-cut.

A Saddle of Mutton.—Cut moderately thick slices, longwise, from the tail to the end, on each side the back-bone; if they be too long, divide them: cut fat from the sides or flaps

---

A Haunch of Mutton—Should be carved as venison.

Loin of Mutton.—Cut the joints into chops and serve them separately; or cut slices the whole length of the loin; or run the knife along the chine-bone, and then slice it, the fat and lean together.

Neck of Mutton.—It should be prepared for table as follows:—Cut off the scrag; have the chine-bone carefully sawn off, and also the top of the long bones (about 1½ inch), and the thin part turned under; carve in the direction of the bones.

The Scrag of Mutton—When roasted, is very frequently separated from the ribs of the neck, and in that case the meat and bones may be helped together.

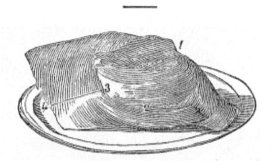

A Fore-Quarter of Lamb.—Cut round the shoulder in the direction of 1, 2, and 3; then lift up the shoulder, and squeeze between it and the ribs the juice of half a lemon, with a slice of butter, some pepper and salt; replace the shoulder, and presently remove it to another dish, to be cut as a shoulder of mutton. Then separate the neck from the ribs, in the line from 3 to 4, and serve according to choice. A ruffle of white paper should be placed round the shank of the shoulder, for the convenience of lifting it while seasoning, &c.

Haunch of Venison.

Haunch of Venison.—Have the joint lengthwise before you, the knuckle being the furthest point. Cut from *a* to *b*, but be careful not to let out the gravy; then cut along the whole length from *a* down to *d*. The knife should slope in making the first cut, and then the whole of the gravy will be received in the well. The greater part of the fat, which is the favorite portion, will be found on the left side, and care must be taken to serve some with each slice.

Pork.—The leg when sent to table should be placed with the back uppermost and the crackling be removed; if sufficiently baked, this may be done with ease; the meat should be served in thin slices cut across the leg, the crackling being served with it, or not, according to taste; the loins are cut into the pieces as scored by the butcher.

Boiled Tongue.—Carve across the tongue, but do not cut through; keep the slices rather thin, and help the fat from underneath.

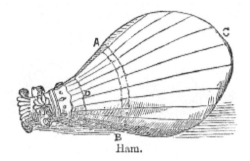

Ham.

Ham—It is served as placed in the engraving, and should come to table ornamented. Carve from A to B, cutting thin slices out slantingly, to give a wedge-like appearance. Those who prefer the *hock* carve at D, in the same direction as from A to B, then carve from D to C, in thin slices, as indicated in the diagram.

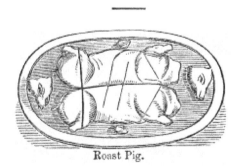

Roast Pig.

Sucking Pig.—The cook should send a roast pig to table as displayed here, garnished with head and ears, carve the joints in the direction shown by the lines in the diagram, then divide the ribs, serve with plenty of sauce; should one of the joints be too much, it may be separated; bread sauce and stuffing should accompany it.

The carving of both *winged game* and *poultry* requires more delicacy of hand and nicety in hitting the joints than the cutting of large pieces of meat, and to be neatly done, requires considerable practice.

Roast Turkey.

Roast Turkey.—Cut long slices from each side of the breast down to the ribs, beginning at *a b* from the wing to the breastbone. If the party be so large as to render it necessary, the legs may then be removed, and the thighs divided from a drum-sticks, which are only served in cases of necessity, as being rather tough, but the pinions of the wing are very savory, and the white part of the wing is preferred by many to the flesh of the breast. The joint of the pinion may be found a little below *b*, and the wing may then be easily removed without touching the leg. The carcase is very seldom dissected, but the body is frequently filled with either truffles, mushrooms, or other matter, in which case an opening must be made into it by cutting a circular incision through the apron, at *c*.

Boiled Turkey.

Boiled Turkey—Is carved in the same way as the roast, the only difference being in the trussing: the legs in the boiled being, as here shown, drawn into the body, and in the roast skewered.

Turkey Poults—Are carved and helped in the same way as pheasants; the stuffing of the grown birds being usually omitted.

A Goose.—Place the neck end towards you, cut the breast into slices, and serve them as cut. If the legs be required, turn the goose upon the side, put the fork into the small end of the bone in the leg, press it to the body, pass the knife in at 4, turn the leg back, and it will easily come off. Next, remove the wing on the same side, by putting the fork into the small end of the pinion, pressing it to the body, dividing the joint at 4, and taking it off in the direction of 3; then turn over the goose, and take off the other leg and wing. Remove the merrythought as from the fowl, and cut off the side-bones by the wing, and the lower side-bones. Divide the breast from the back, and the back itself, as of a fowl. Next to the breast, the thigh and the fleshy portion of the wing are favorite parts. If the goose be not entirely cut up, the apron, 1, 2, should be removed to get at the stuffing.

A Duck—Should be cut up as a goose.

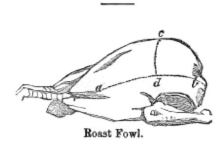

Roast Fowl.

Roast Fowl.—Slip the knife between the leg and body, and cut to the bone; then with the fork turn the leg back, and the joint will give way if the bird is not old. Take the wing off in the direction of *a* to *b*, only dividing the joint with your knife. When the four quarters are thus removed, take off the merry thought from *c*, and the neck-bones; these last, by putting in the knife at *d*, and pressing it, will break off from the part that sticks to the breast. The next thing is to divide the breast from the carcase, by cutting through the tender ribs close to the breast, quite down to the tail. Then lay the back upwards, put your knife into the bone half way from the neck to the rump, and on raising the lower end it will separate readily. Turn the rump from you, take off the two sidesmen, and the whole will be done. To separate the thigh from the drumstick of the leg insert the knife into the joint as above. It requires practice to hit the joint at the first trial. The breast and wings are considered the best parts.

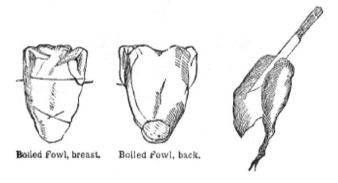

Boiled fowl, breast.   Boiled fowl, back.

If the bird be a capon, or large and roasted, the breast may be cut into slices in the same way as a pheasant.

The difference in the carving of boiled and roast fowls consists only in the breast of the latter being always served whole, and the thigh-bone being generally preferred to the wing.

A Partridge—Is to be cut up as a fowl: take off the wings in the lines 1, 2, and the merrythought in that of 3, 4. Partridges may likewise be cut in half. The prime parts are the breast and wings, the tip of the latter being the greatest delicacy.

Printed in the USA
CPSIA information can be obtained
at www.ICGtesting.com
LVHW071953140124
768898LV00080BA/2171